The Battle of Bull Run
Confederate Forces Overwhelm Union Troops

Wendy Vierow

The Rosen Publishing Group's
PowerKids Press™
New York

For John, Judy, Theresa, and Nicholas

Published in 2004 by The Rosen Publishing Group, Inc.
29 East 21st Street, New York, NY 10010

First Edition

Editor: Frances E. Ruffin
Book Design: Michael de Guzman

Photo Credits: Cover (inset) North Wind Picture Archives, cover photo (rifle) Photo by Peter Latner, Minnesota Historical Society, (hats) Cindy Reiman; pp. 4, 5, 6, 8, 9, 11, 17, 19, 21 Library of Congress, Prints and Photographs Division; pp. 7, 13 © Bettmann/CORBIS; p. 12, 15 © Hulton/Archive/Getty Images; p. 20 Print Collection, Miriam and Ira D. Wallach Division of Art, Prints and Photographs, The New York Public Library, Astor, Lenox and Tilden Foundations.

Vierow, Wendy.
The Battle of Bull Run : Confederate forces overwhelm Union troops /Wendy Vierow.— 1st ed.
    p. cm. — (Headlines from history)
Includes bibliographical references and index.
  ISBN 0-8239-6221-0
1. Bull Run, 1st Battle of, Va., 1861—Juvenile literature. [1. Bull Run, 1st Battle of, Va., 1861. 2. United States—History—Civil War, 1861–1865—Campaigns.] I. Title. II. Series.
  E472.18 .V54 2003
  973.7'31—dc21
                                                                                          2001005470

Manufactured in the United States of America

CONTENTS

1 The United States Enters a Civil War   4

2 Men Sign Up as Soldiers   6

3 Troops Arrive to Fight   8

4 Union Troops March to Manassas   10

5 The Battle Begins   12

6 The Union Retreats   14

7 Slaves Escape North   16

8 Lincoln Fears Losing the Border States   18

9 General McClellan Trains Union Troops   20

10 A New Type of War   22

Glossary   23

Index   24

Primary Sources   24

Web Sites   24

The United States Enters a Civil War

The first battle of Bull Run began on July 21, 1861, 100 days after the South fired shots on U.S. troops at Fort Sumter in South Carolina. This first battle of Bull Run lasted for one day. A second battle at Bull Run began on August 29, 1862, and was fought for two days.

The shots at Fort Sumter started the **Civil War**. The main reason for the Civil War was a disagreement between the people of Northern and Southern states about **slavery**. Most Northerners thought that slavery was wrong. Most Southerners thought that slavery should be allowed. Those Southerners argued that without

This map shows the Union states colored purple, the Confederate states colored orange, and the border states colored brown.

Abraham Lincoln is shown here without his well-known beard.

Jefferson Davis was a former Mississippi state senator.

the free labor of slaves, they would not be able to run their large farms, or plantations. By the end of 1861, 11 Southern states had formed their own country, called the **Confederate States of America**. The **Union** had 23 states. The president of the Confederacy was Jefferson Davis. The president of the United States was Abraham Lincoln. Both men were born in Kentucky. Both men were dedicated to their own causes.

SECESSION
1860 · 1861

Men Sign Up as Soldiers

When war broke out, men rushed to sign up to fight for either the Confederacy or the Union. Almost everyone thought the war would be finished quickly.

Some men had to make difficult choices about which side to join. A Virginian called General Robert E. Lee did not agree with **secession**. However, when Virginia left the Union, he chose to join the Confederacy. He said, "I cannot raise my hand against my birthplace, my home, and my children."

Before the Civil War, Robert E. Lee was a well-respected general in the U.S. Army. The decision to join the Confederate army in his home state was a difficult one.

Some soldiers who signed up to fight for the Union ran into trouble before even seeing a battle. Angry crowds in Baltimore, Maryland, who supported the Confederacy, attacked Union soldiers from Massachusetts who were marching through the city to Washington, D.C. Four soldiers and nine citizens were killed.

Some soldiers had lost their belongings during the march. When the Union soldiers reached Washington, D.C., a woman named Clara Barton and her friends gave the soldiers supplies from their homes.

Clara Barton, a government worker, served as a volunteer during the Civil War. She later went on to start the Red Cross in the United States.

Troops Arrive to Fight

As men gathered to fight for either the Union or the Confederacy, it became clear that things were not very organized. At the time, neither side had enough formal uniforms for its soldiers. Union soldiers from Minnesota arrived in flannel shirts and black pants. Some Union soldiers from New York wore gray, the color of the Confederate uniform. The Union soldiers camped in the U.S. Capitol building. They practiced drilling in the park.

Union soldiers, like the one pictured here, often wore blue uniforms. They were sometimes called the Blues.

Confederate soldiers, like the one shown here, often wore gray uniforms and were called the Grays. 👉

The Confederate soldiers also wore a variety of uniforms. Some Confederate troops arrived wearing blue, the color of the Union uniform.

Most men who fought in the Civil War had little fighting experience. Many Southerners, who were farmers, at least knew how to fire a gun, to ride a horse, and to work outdoors. Men on both sides fought in their army's **cavalry**, **artillery**, or **infantry**. Most fought as foot soldiers in the infantry.

Union Troops March to Manassas

The Confederate capital, Richmond, Virginia, was only 100 miles (161 km) from Washington, D.C., the capital of the United States. Manassas, Virginia, lay between the two cities. By mid July, Confederate troops had gathered at Manassas **Junction**. At this location, they were in a good position either to defend Richmond or to attack Washington, D.C.

In Washington, D.C., people became restless. They wanted Union troops to capture the Confederate capital of Richmond and to end the war. On July 16, 1861, Union troops left Washington, D.C., and marched toward

Here some Union troops cross Sudley Ford on horseback before the first battle of Bull Run in July 1861.

Manassas. It took them two and a half days to get to Manassas. The soldiers were not used to marching for long distances. They stopped to pick berries, to drink water, and to rest.

On July 21, the battle finally began. People came to watch the battle. Many had even traveled from Washington, D.C., in fancy carriages. They brought picnic lunches and **binoculars**.

Most people thought this one battle would decide who would win the war.

The Battle Begins

"Stonewall" Jackson was successful in holding off the Union attack at the first battle of Bull Run. He was killed in a battle accident in 1863.

Soldiers on both sides were shocked when the fighting began in Manassas on July 21, 1861. Neither side was prepared for the confusion that followed. The lack of formal uniforms made it hard for soldiers on both sides to identify the enemy.

Brigadier General Irvin McDowell led Union troops. General Pierre Gustave Toutant Beauregard and General Joseph E. Johnston led Confederate troops. During the battle, the Confederate troops led by Thomas J. Jackson held their ground. Because his soldiers stood firm, Jackson got the nickname Stonewall Jackson. Jackson also told his troops to yell while fighting. This is the first time that Union soldiers, called **Yankees**, heard the **rebel** yell. Confederate soldiers made this yell in

12

This is a scene from the first battle that took place at Manassas, or Bull Run. The confusion of the battle comes through very clearly in this painting.

battle. It sounded like a shout and a yelp. Toward the end of the battle, Confederate president Jefferson Davis rode out to watch.

At Manassas there was a stream called Bull Run. The Union usually named battles after landmarks or waterways. The Confederacy named battles after nearby towns or railroad stations.

The Union Retreats

Union soldiers were getting tired by late afternoon on the day of the battle. Many soldiers began to leave the battlefield, but the Confederates kept fighting. Soon the Union soldiers began to panic. Many Union soldiers dropped their weapons and began to run back to Washington, D.C., afraid that the Confederates were chasing them.

Citizens who watched the battle also panicked. When they saw that the Union was losing, citizens left their picnic spots and ran to their carriages. Carriages soon blocked the roads. The Confederates were too confused to pursue the Union army. The next day, Confederates gathered the weapons, the horses, and the swords left by Union soldiers.

A Union supply train, shown here in a watercolor painting, is retreating from the battle at Bull Run.

Union troops poured back into Washington, D.C. Many soldiers were wounded and dying. Clara Barton, who went on to nurse men on Civil War battlefields, helped the wounded as they arrived in Washington, D.C. The **casualties** from the battle of Bull Run were high. About 3,000 Union soldiers and 2,000 Confederate soldiers were either killed, missing, or wounded.

Slaves Escape North

Weeks after the first battle of Bull Run, thousands of slaves escaped to the North. Many approached the Union army. U.S. law stated that slaves had to be returned to their owners, but many Union officers thought that the law was wrong. A Union officer called General Benjamin Butler asked politicians in Washington, D.C., to allow escaped slaves to stay in the North. He argued that because the Confederacy claimed to be a different country, the law should not apply.

The United States passed a law that allowed officers to free slaves aiding the Confederacy. Soon many African Americans who escaped from slavery went to work for the Union army.

Former slaves approached the Union army wishing to help in some way. They were not allowed to fight at the beginning of the war but helped in other ways.

Although they were not yet allowed to fight in the army, they helped by digging ditches, cooking, and washing clothes. African Americans were helping the Union to win the war.

Lincoln Fears Losing the Border States

After the Union lost the first battle of Bull Run, President Lincoln worried that the border states might leave the Union. The Union's border states, Delaware, Maryland, Kentucky, and Missouri, allowed slavery. These states were called border states because they bordered the North and the South.

Washington, D.C., the capital of the United States, was surrounded by states that allowed slavery. If Maryland joined the Confederacy, Washington, D.C., would be surrounded by Confederate states. President Lincoln had Maryland politicians who supported the Confederacy put in jail. New politicians were elected, and Maryland remained with the Union.

President Lincoln also worried that Kentucky would **secede**. If Kentucky joined the Confederacy, the Confederacy would have more supplies and would control the Ohio and the Mississippi Rivers. This would prevent Union troops from traveling through Kentucky by river. When Confederate troops invaded Kentucky in September 1861, politicians there became angry and turned to Union troops to drive out the Confederates. Kentucky stayed with the Union.

Massachusetts's volunteers are shown here fighting in the streets of Baltimore, Maryland, as they march to defend the capital in Washington, D.C.

General McClellan Trains Union Troops

After losing the first battle of Bull Run, President Lincoln chose a new leader for the Union army. General George B. McClellan arrived in Washington, D.C., on July 26, 1861, with plans to train Union troops. McClellan set new rules for soldiers. They had to have passes to leave camp. Soldiers who walked around Washington, D.C., without a pass were arrested.

McClellan also made the soldiers **drill** often so that they would be prepared to fight in battle. They learned to march and to use their guns. After drilling they had to do chores, such

After McClellan took charge of the Union army, the Union soldiers worked hard. Here the Union soldiers are resting after drills.

This is a portrait of General George B. McClellan.

Most of the photographs that we have of the Civil War were taken by Mathew Brady and the men who worked for him.

as caring for horses, building paths, and repairing equipment. They also had to watch for enemies. Soldiers learned **obedience** so that they would be able to obey orders in battle. Soldiers who disobeyed orders were punished. They could be sent to prison or be forced to do something embarrassing, such as marching while carrying a log. The days of easy camp life were finished.

A New Type of War

The Civil War was different from other wars in history. In the first battle of Bull Run, the Confederate army used the railroad to bring troops quickly to battle. This was the first time that this had ever been done in a war. By using railroads, troops could arrive at the battle rested and ready to fight. After the first battle of Bull Run, both sides used railroads. The Union had better railroads than did the South, which helped it to win the war.

Americans got to see photographs of the war. A photographer named Mathew Brady followed Union and Confederate troops to make a record of the Civil War for the public. Many new inventions were used, including iron warships, **submarines**, and **telegraphs** that sent messages over a distance. The Civil War was the world's first modern war.

GLOSSARY

artillery (ar-TIH-luhr-ee) The part of an army that uses large guns, such as cannons.

binoculars (bih-NA-kyuh-lurz) Handheld lenses that make things seem clearer.

casualties (KA-zhul-teez) People who are injured or killed in an accident or a war.

cavalry (KA-vul-ree) The part of an army that rides horses.

Civil War (SIH-vul WOR) The war fought between the Northern and the Southern states of America from 1861 to 1865.

Confederate States of America (kun-FEH-duh-ret STAYTZ UV uh-MER-ih-kuh) A group of 11 Southern states that declared themselves separate from the United States in 1860–1861.

drill (DRIL) To teach someone something by having them do the thing over and over again.

infantry (IN-fun-tree) The part of an army that walks while fighting.

junction (JUNG-shun) A place where roads or railroad tracks meet or join.

obedience (oh-BEE-dee-ents) The act of doing what one is told to do.

rebel (REH-bul) A person who fought for the South during the Civil War.

secede (sih-SEED) To withdraw from a group or a country.

secession (sih-SEH-shun) The act of withdrawing from a group or a country.

slavery (SLAY-vuh-ree) The system of people "owned" by and forced to work for other people.

submarines (SUHB-muh-reenz) Ships that are designed to travel underwater.

telegraphs (TEH-luh-grafs) The equipment or systems for sending messages over long distances with electrical codes sent by wire or by radio.

Union (YOON-yun) The Northern states during the Civil War.

Yankees (YAN-keez) People who fought for the North during the Civil War.

23

INDEX

B

Barton, Clara, 7, 15

border states, 18

Butler, General Benjamin, 16

C

Civil War, 4, 9, 15, 22

D

Davis, Jefferson, 5, 13

F

Fort Sumter, 4

J

Jackson, Thomas J., 12

L

Lee, General Robert E., 6

Lincoln, Abraham, 5, 18–20

M

Manassas Junction, 10–13

McClellan, General George B., 20

R

rebel yell, 12

Richmond, Virginia, 10

S

slave(s), 5, 16

U

uniform(s), 8–9, 12

W

Washington, D.C., 7, 10–11, 14–16, 18, 20

Y

Yankees, 12

PRIMARY SOURCES

Page 4: Lithograph of a clean-shaven Abraham Lincoln by F. D'Avignon. From the Library of Congress; **Page 5 (top)**: A hand-colored lithograph of Jefferson Davis, created between 1850 and 1870 by Blelock and Co.; **(bottom)** Map of the United States showing the secession of the southern states, 1860–1861 by Albert Bushnell Hart (1917); **Page 6**: Portrait of Confederate General Robert E. Lee, photographed by Julian Vannerson (1863); **Page 7**: Clara Barton, from the U.S. Army Office of the Chief Signal Officer. Photographed in the Washington Gallery by Mathew Brady (1866); **Page 8**: Photograph of a federal soldier from Ohio (1860–1865); **Page 9**: Photograph of a confederate soldier (1860–1865); **Page 11**: Photograph of federal cavalry at Sudley Ford in Bull Run, Virginia. Taken by George N. Barnard (July, 1861); **Page 12**: Photograph of General Stonewall Jackson by the New York Photographic Company (1860); **Page 13**: Color lithograph of the first battle of Bull Run, July 21, 1861; **Page 15**: Watercolor painting by William T. Trego of "the great skedaddle"—a Union supply train retreating from Bull Run on the road to Washington, D.C.; **Page 17**: A drawing of a party of slaves moving toward Union lines by Edwin Forbes (1876); **Page 19**: *The Lexington of 1861* a hand-colored lithograph of Massachusetts Volunteers in the Union army fighting in the streets of Baltimore on march to defense of the U.S. Capitol; by Currier and Ives (1861); **Page 20**: Hand-colored lithograph of General George B. McClellan; by Currier and Ives, from the collections of the New York Public Library; **Page 21 (top)**: Photograph of Mathew Brady's photo outfit in front of Petersburg, Virginia (1864); **Page 21 (bottom)**: Photograph of Union infantry resting from drills. War Department, U.S. Army, Office of the Chief Signal Officer. Photograph by Mathew Brady Studio (1860–1865).

WEB SITES

To learn more about The Battle of Bull Run, check out this Web site:
www.civilwarhome.com/1manassa.htm